W9-AXM-539

PARROTS TALK!

Hello!
Hello!

Hello!
Hello!

Pam Scheunemann

Consulting Editor, Diane Craig, M.A./Reading Specialist

A Division of ABDO

ABDO
Publishing Company

visit us at www.abdopublishing.com

Published by ABDO Publishing Company, a division of ABDO, P.O. Box 398166, Minneapolis, Minnesota 55439. Copyright © 2011 by Abdo Consulting Group, Inc. International copyrights reserved in all countries. No part of this book may be reproduced in any form without written permission from the publisher. SandCastle™ is a trademark and logo of ABDO Publishing Company.

Printed in the United States of America, North Mankato, Minnesota
102010
012011

 PRINTED ON RECYCLED PAPER

Editor: Liz Salzmann
Content Developer: Nancy Tuminelly
Cover and Interior Design and Production: Oona Gaarder-Juntti, Mighty Media, Inc.
Photo Credits: Shutterstock

Library of Congress Cataloging-in-Publication Data
Scheunemann, Pam, 1955-
  Parrots talk! / Pam Scheunemann.
    p. cm. -- (Animal sounds)
  ISBN 978-1-61613-574-4
  1. Parrots--Vocalization--Juvenile literature. 2. Talking birds--Juvenile literature. I. Title.
  QL696.P7S34 2011
  636.6'865--dc22
                        2010018752

SandCastle™ Level: Transitional

SandCastle™ books are created by a team of professional educators, reading specialists, and content developers around five essential components—phonemic awareness, phonics, vocabulary, text comprehension, and fluency—to assist young readers as they develop reading skills and strategies and increase their general knowledge. All books are written, reviewed, and leveled for guided reading, early reading intervention, and Accelerated Reader® programs for use in shared, guided, and independent reading and writing activities to support a balanced approach to literacy instruction. The SandCastle™ series has four levels that correspond to early literacy development. The levels are provided to help teachers and parents select appropriate books for young readers.

Emerging Readers
(no flags)

Beginning Readers
(1 flag)

Transitional Readers
(2 flags)

Fluent Readers
(3 flags)

contents

Parrots come in many colors, such as yellow, blue, and red.

Some squawk and some talk when they want to be fed!

Not all parrots eat the same kind of food. A parrot's diet can include seeds, fruit, nuts, buds, and nectar.

A parrot has a hard, curved beak.

Parrots use their beaks to get food and defend themselves.

Some types of parrots learn to speak.

African gray parrots are thought to be the best talkers.

Parrots hold their perches with their toes.

A parrot has four toes on each foot. Two toes point forward, and two toes point backward.

This parrot has been in many shows!

Parrots are smart birds.
They can learn to do tricks.

Parrots keep their feathers clean.

Bathing is important for parrots. It keeps their skin from becoming dry and itchy.

They often take the time to preen!

Parrots use their beaks to pick dirt out of their feathers. They may even help their friends preen!

Parrots sure do like to play.

Parrots need toys to keep them from being bored. Toys also help them get the exercise they need.

Be kind to your parrot every day.

Larger parrots can live up to 75 years. They need attention from their owners. They like to be part of the family!

You never know what it will say!